Ultrasound Analysis for Condition Monitoring

Applications of Ultrasound Detection for Various Industrial Equipment

Mohammed Hamed Ahmed Soliman

CONTENTS

Introduction to Ultrasound Technique 4

Overview on the Instrument 9

Typical Applications 11

Ultrasound For Condition Monitoring 30

Case Study 34

Ultrasonic Condition-Based Lubrication...........................39

Machine Faults Detection Using Ultrasound.....................49

Ultrasound and Medical Field 50

References...52

About the Author..53

INTRODUCTION TO
ULTRASOUND TECHNIQUE

What is Ultrasound?
Ultrasound is
cyclic sound pressure with
a frequency greater than the upper limit
of human hearing, excess of 20,000 cycles
(hertz) per second (20KHZ).

So, by definition, ultrasound is totally
undetectable by human ears unless aided by
instruments capable of translating ultrasound
to audible sound. In the marketplace, these
instruments are commonly known as
ultrasonic detectors and have been used for
various maintenance related functions for
over 25 years.

Ultrasonic is a predictive maintenance
technique and one of the non-destructive
testing tools that used in the field of industry
to detect early & hidden equipment failures.

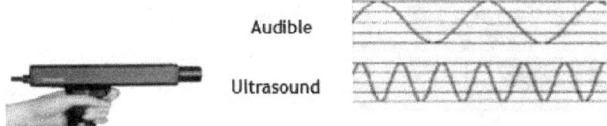

Audible

Ultrasound

What is the Different between Ultrasonic & Vibration?

Vibration is a low frequency method that can detect bearing failures and the reason of this failure.

Ultrasonic is a high frequency vibration method (ultrasonic vibration) that can detect the degrees of bearing failures & wears, it can also detect the lubrication problems of the bearing.

One of the most advantages of using ultrasonic over vibration, is that ultrasonic can reveal the lubrication problems and provide a very early warning of bearing faults.

The very early detection of bearing failure using ultrasound can save a lot of money and equipment life; preventing unexpected plant stop and loss of productivity.

Ultrasound should be a part of any predictive maintenance planning program.

Type of fault	Vibration	Temp	Oil
Out of balance	xxx	----	----
Misalignment	xxx	x	----
Damage of bearing	xxx	xx	x
Damage of gear box	xxx	x	xx
Belt problems	xx	----	----
Motor problems	xx	x	----
Mechanical looseness	xxx	x	x
Resonance	xxx	----	----

Vibration VS Thermography VS Oil Analysis

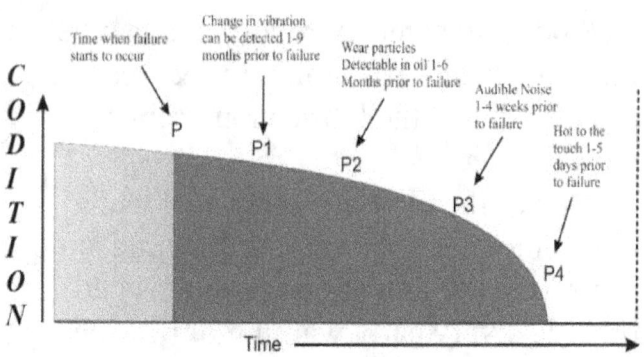

Stages at which failure occurs.

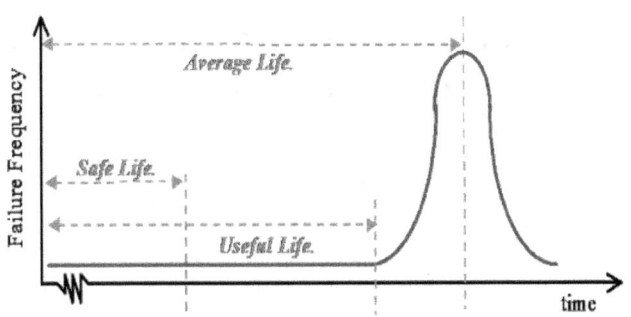

Determines equipment life time and its parts changing frequency.

Predictive Maintenance Embraced by Plant Maintenance

Technique	Application	Pumps	Electric Motors	Diesel Generators	Condensers	Heavy Equipment/ Crane	Circuit Breakers	Valves	Heat Exchangers	Electrical Systems	Transformers	Tank Piping
VIB Analysis		•	•	•		•						
Oil Analysis		•	•	•		•					•	
Wear Analysis		•	•	•		•						
IR Analysis		•	•	•	•	•	•	•	•	•	•	
Ultrasound		•	•	•	•		•	•	•	•	•	
Non-Destructive testing (Thickness)					•			•			•	
Visual Inspection		•	•	•	•	•	•	•	•	•	•	•
Motor Current Analysis		•										

Should we run an expensive diagnosis for all systems and equipment in the plant?

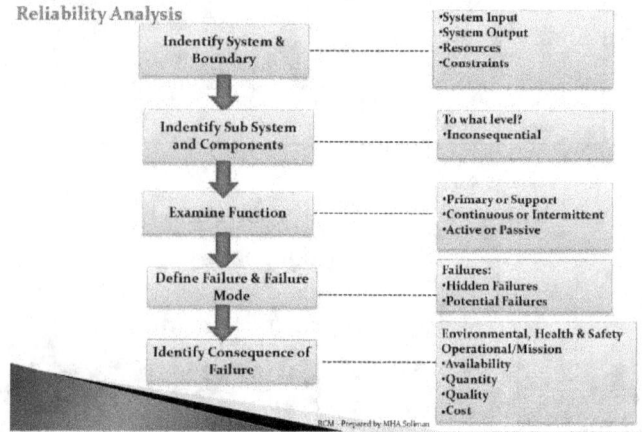

Reliability analysis provide a guidance for where, when, and how to apply condition monitoring.

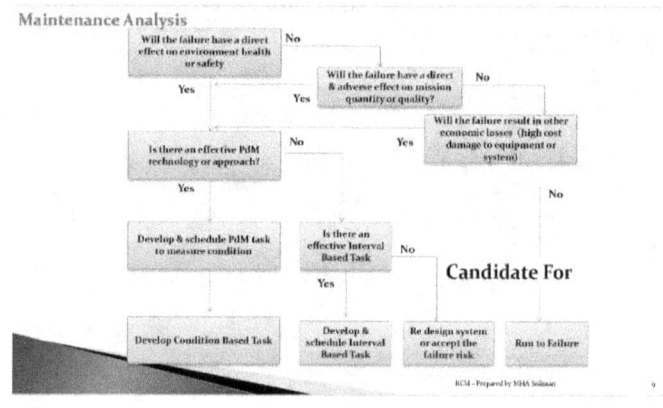

Reliability analysis

OVERVIEW ON THE INSTRUMENT

1 **. Ultrasound Detector**
Lightweight and portable, ultrasonic translators are often used to inspect a wide variety of equipment. Some helpful accessories are supplied with the instrument too.

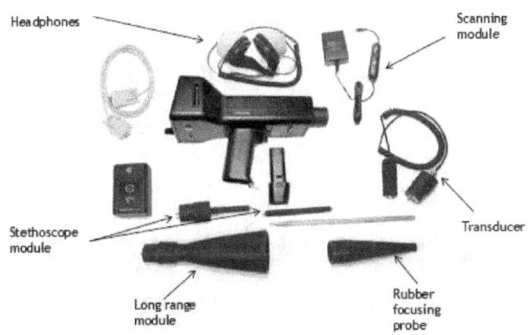

This is called Ultraprobe, available in different type for wide range of uses.

2. Remote Sensors
Remote Monitoring Sensors has many applications and uses especially in bearing, lubrication, and grease monitoring.

3. Software
Used for analysis and reporting

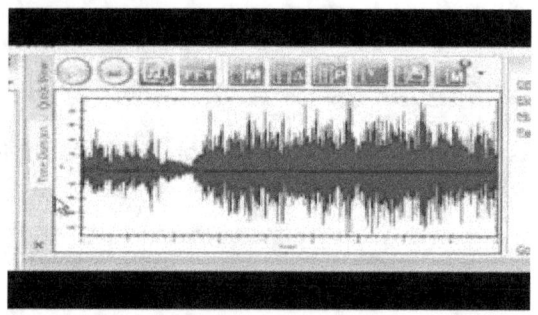

M. echanical Equipment and Process Inspection

- PRESSURE/VACUUM LEAKS (TURBULENCE)
- COMPRESSED AIR
- OXYGEN
- HYDROGEN ETC.
- HEAT EXCHANGERS
- BOILERS
- CONDENSERS
- TANKS
- PIPES
- VALVES
- STEAM TRAPS
- MECHANICAL INSPECTION
- BEARINGS
- LACK OF LUBRICATION/FAILURE
- PUMPS

- MOTORS
- GEARS/GEAR BOXES
- FANS
- COMPRESSORS
- CONVEYERS
- AUTOMOTIVE
- RAIL ROADS
- MARINE
- AVIATION
- ELECTRIC EQUIPMENT
- (Arcing/tracking/corona)
- SWITCHGEAR
- TRANSFORMERS
- INSULATORS
- POTHEADS
- JUNCTION BOXES
- CIRCUIT BREAKERS

Leak Detection

Reasons for using Ultrasound to detect leaks:

1. Economics
2. Environmental
3. Safety

Economics: Save energy.

Environmental: Slowing global climate change by limiting gases emissions and leaks.

Social/Safety: Less harmful air pollution can improve the health of employees and the general public.

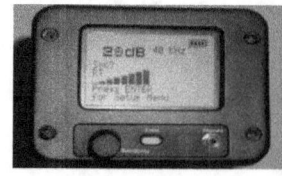

Locate the leak.

Measure the leak.

Calculate costs.

Calculate greenhouse gas emission reduction.

Ultrasonic Valves Leak Detection

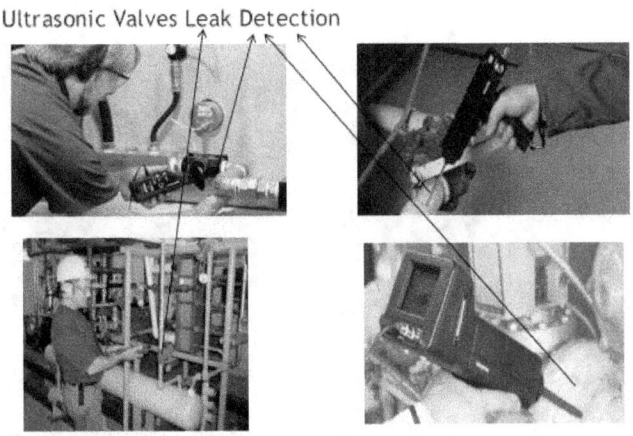

Good Valve – Bad Valve

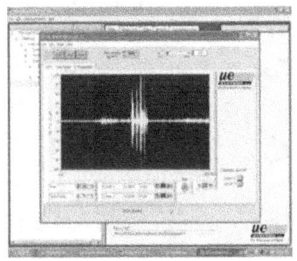 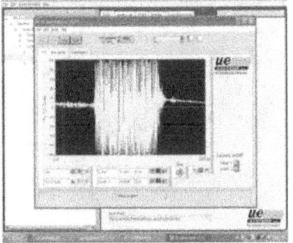

Detect Boiler leakage

Detect Heat Exchanger Leakage

Detect Steam Trap Leakage

Detect Steam Traps Leakage

Detect Condenser Leakage

Detect Tanks Leakage

Steam spills are additionally among the most inefficient, and in this manner, costly issues found in a plant. Truth be told, spilling steam traps can increment working costs by as much as 33 percent. Hence, energy preservation projects should begin with a steam trap study.

As per the Department of Energy's Office of Energy Efficiency and Renewable Energy, even the littlest steam trap hole can cost up to $8,000 every year. A dry steam spill costs $15 per each thousand pounds.

Some Tips to Reduce Steam Leaks
From various perspectives, steam holes can be very like compacted air spills. For this reason, directing a study like packed air is an incredible method to ensure your steam framework is routinely kept up.
It's imperative to watch out for the primary driver for steam spills furthermore, their answers.
1. Strung line associations: Pipe strings can come up short as they extend furthermore, contract with steam and buildup.

» Instead, utilize an alternate type of association, for example, welded or tube-type associations.

2. Pressing on standard kind valves: Standard pressing on steam separation valves are inclined to breakdown without a careful proactive support program.
» Ball valves and butterfly valves can all the more likely location these fixing issues.

3. Carbonic Acid: Carbonic corrosive can separate the absolute weakest pieces of a steam framework.
» By utilizing more grounded association strategies, for example, welded or tube types, frameworks can more readily oppose consumption, while utilizing spotless steel will improve the opposition of the condensate framework.

Detect Compressor Leakage and Air Valves

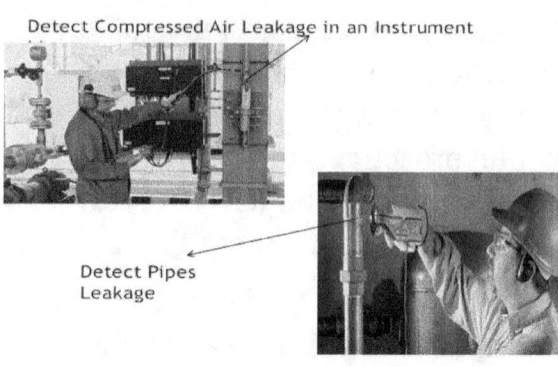

Detect Compressed Air Leakage in an Instrument

Detect Pipes Leakage

Air Leakage

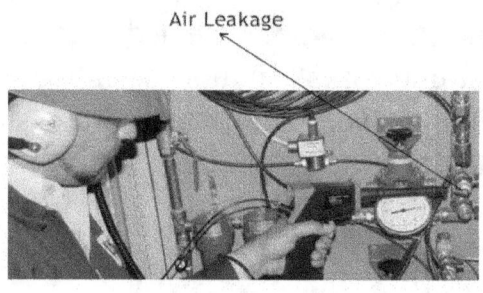

Do you know how much does leak cost in a compressed air network?! The energy consumption?

In 1995, 30 percent of all industrial compressed air was lost to leaks, resulting in around approximately $3.2 billion in losses (UE Systems, Energy Book).

Coming up next are the four significant parts of actualizing a compacted air spill recognition review:

1. Make a course for assessment based around the plan of your air funneling framework.
» Make sure to discover and label all breaks. Watch out for abuse, for example, valves that are left all the way open.

2. Plan the most ideal course for review
» Start from the blower/flexibly side and work toward the utilization side each an ideal opportunity to look after consistency.
» Take a sketch or chart of your framework to assist you with recognizing all the segments of the framework.
» Break your way into a progression of zones that can make your assessment course more coordinated and simpler to follow.

3. Follow a similar course each time so you don't miss any parts during your review
» Use ultrasound to get little breaks before they become bigger issues.

4. Label your distinguished breaks and report your outcomes to the board, featuring your expense and energy reserve funds.

Simply by implementing these steps into their reliability programs, every plant could reduce its energy waste by 10 to 20 percent.

Bearings problems can be detected in any type of equipment using ultrasound

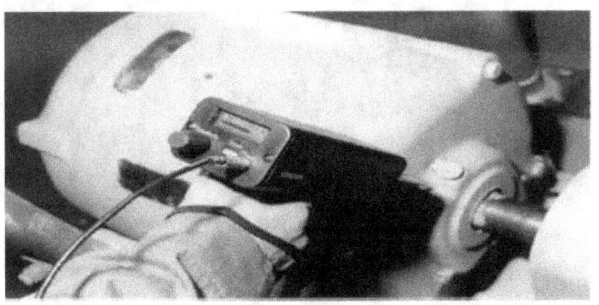

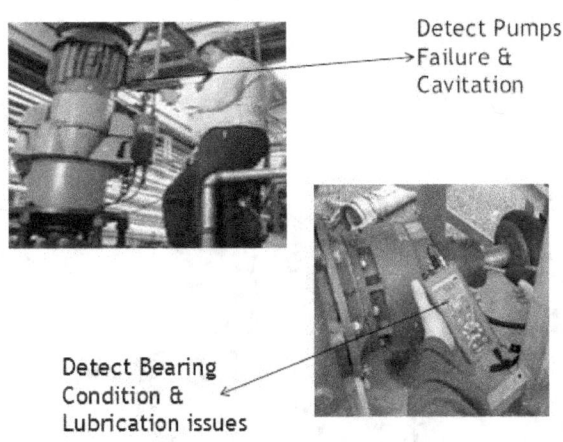

Detect Pumps
→Failure &
Cavitation

Detect Bearing
Condition &
Lubrication issues

Electric Inspection

CORONA

TRACKING

ARCING

Ultrasound is Good for MEDIUM and HIGH
Voltage

Circuit Breakers

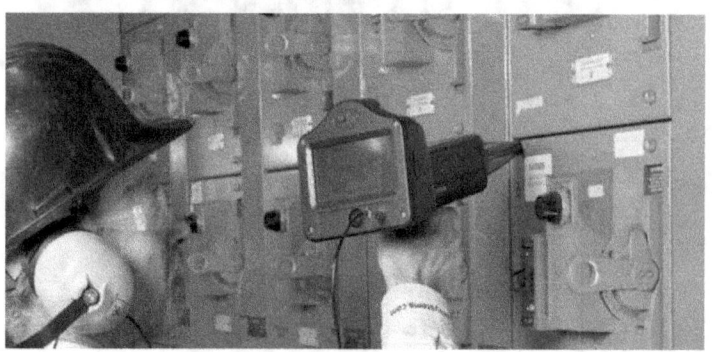

Transformer Issues: bushing, winding, oil, cooling system, condenser

Electric Discharges:
Arcing
Corona
Tracking

Detect Gearbox Broken Teeth

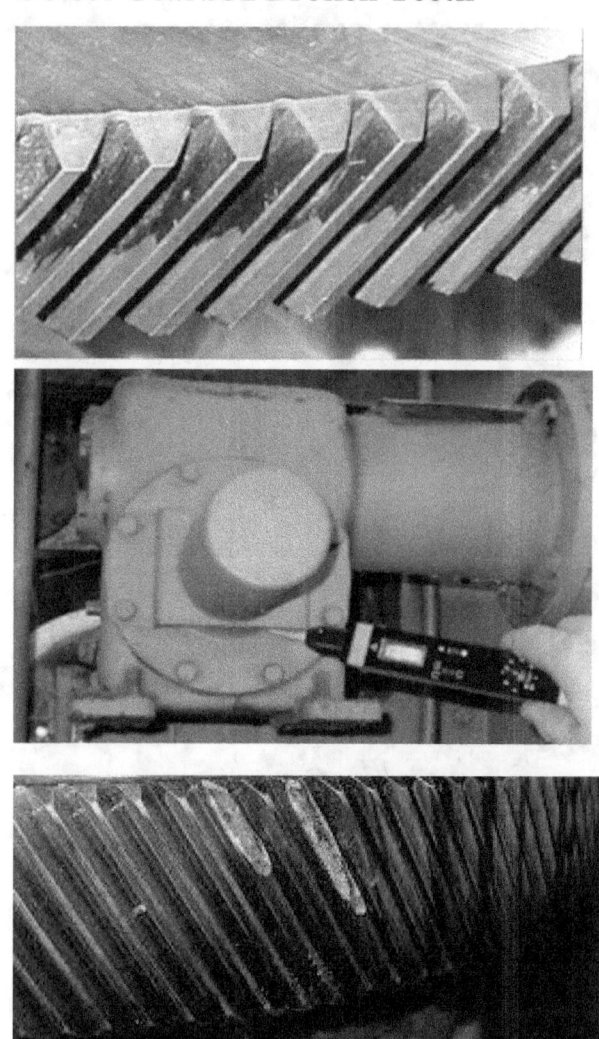

Employing Ultrasonic or Eddy Current Inspection of Turbine Blades: Ensuring Flight Safety

Aerospace Inspection

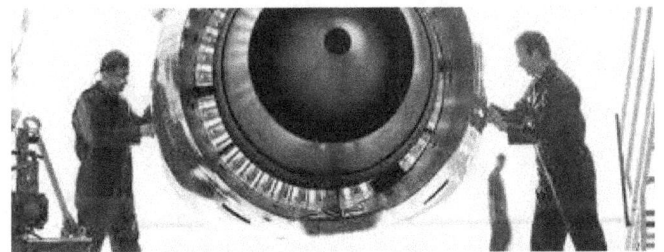

Aviation Inspection

In Automotive Industry

Ultrasonic leak detector inspects doors and windows sealed air noise leakage hatch cover detection.

ULTRASOUND FOR CONDITION MONITORING

Ultrasound technique has some advantages and disadvantages when it comes to machine condition monitoring.

Advantages

1. Ultrasound emissions are directional.
2. Ultrasound tends to be highly localized.
3. Ultrasound provides early warning of impending mechanical failure.
4. The instruments can be used in loud, noisy environments.
5. They support and enhance other PDM technologies or can stand on their own in a maintenance program.
6. Test hazard equipment from long distances.
7. Discover early failures without stopping the equipment.

Disadvantages

1. Surface to be tested must be ground smooth and clean
2. Skilled and trained operator is required.
3. Quite expensive method.

How the ultrasound instrument works?
If we want to listen to ultrasound, we need an instrument capable of translating high frequencies into a range we can hear (normally 200-5000 hertz is a comfortable listening range). That is the function of an ultrasound detector. If we want to listen ONLY to ultrasound, we need a detector with certain filters to eliminate audible or "parasite" noises. If we want to measure the energy of the ultrasound then the detector should have digital measurement capabilities.

This equipment can usually store the measurements to an onboard memory chip and transmit the data to PC software.

Measurement of the Signal

Ultrasonic or acoustic vibration is energy created by the friction between moving components (bearings, couplings, gear mesh, etc…). This energy is really an AC voltage or current that is at best, highly unstable and erratic. To provide useful data for acoustic vibration monitoring this energy must be made linear for repeatability purposes. A quality ultrasonic detector uses True RMS conversion techniques to accomplish this. RMS means "Root Mean Squared." It's a way of measuring an AC voltage by means of taking the root of mean squared samples. Basically, True RMS measurement is a technique that provides consistent theoretically valid measurements of electrical signals derived from mechanical phenomena such as strain, stress, vibration, shock, expansion, bearing noise, and acoustic vibration.

The electrical signals produced by these mechanical actions are often noisy, non-periodic, and non-sinusoidal, superimposed on DC levels, and require True RMS for, valid, accurate, and repeatable measurements.

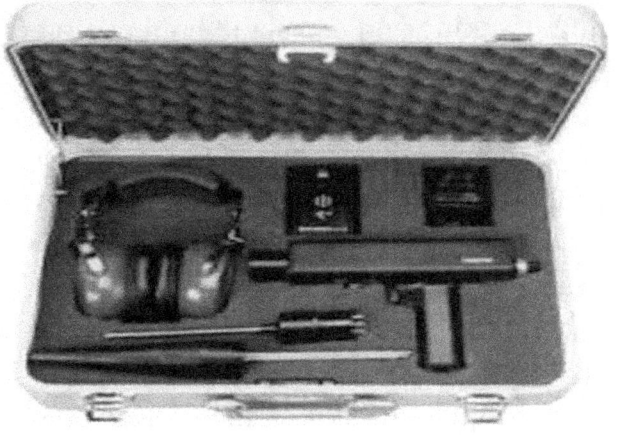

Ultrasound innovation is an amazingly helpful apparatus with regards to actualizing a quality improvement program. This is on the grounds that it can distinguish issues with machines before they become bigger issues. By distinguishing commotion that would somehow or another be imperceptible to the human ear, ultrasound attempts to recognize issues before they become exorbitant and tedious to fix.

Electric Emissions (Case Study Switch Gear inside Cabinet) Ultrasound inspection works on all voltages, low, medium and high to detect arcing, tracking and corona in both enclosed and open access equipment. Arcing, tracking and corona ionize the air molecules around them, which produces ultrasound. With the advantage of digital sound recording and spectral analysis, inspectors can analyze sound samples to determine the type and severity of an electric emission. Below are some examples of corona, tracking and arcing. As you will note in the FFT screen as the condition becomes more severe, there are fewer harmonics of 60 cycles. If this were in Europe, we would see the same with harmonics of 50 cycles. The first image is Corona (Figure 1) followed by Tracking.

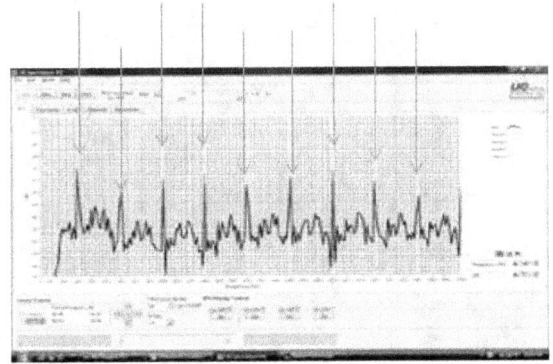

Corona

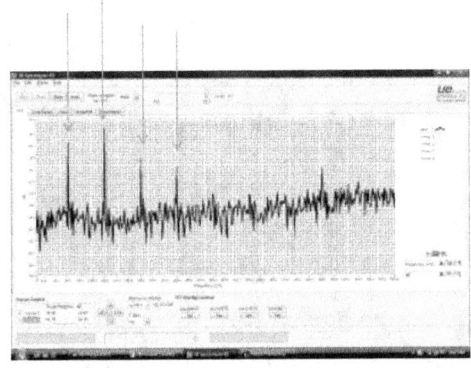

Tracking

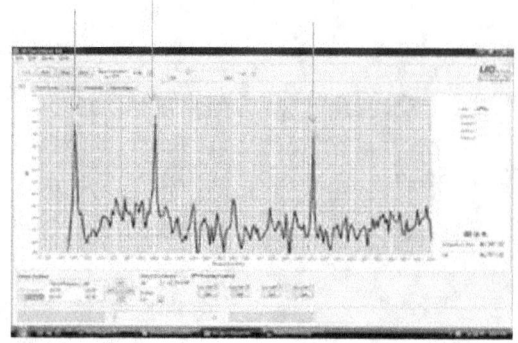

Tracking

The following demonstrate the effectiveness of ultrasound when used with infrared. An inspector who utilizes both ultrasound and infrared technologies was inspecting switchgear. Some of the doors could not be opened. There were no IR ports on the closed cabinets and therefore this switchgear could not be tested with infrared. By scanning the door seams and air vents with the ultrasound instrument, the inspector heard a very distinctive arcing sound. He recorded the sound and after the cabinets were opened, he took visual and infrared images. Below are the results.

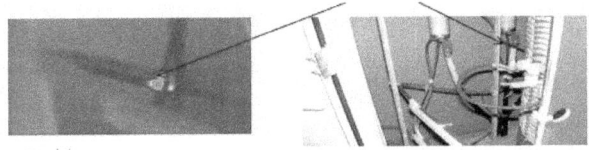

Conclusion

In extreme closed cabinet, Ultrasound beats Thermal Analysis, especially if it's not easy to open the device.

Tips:

What is Corona?

Corona refers to the faint glow surrounding an electrical conductor of 3500 volts or greater as a result of the ionization of air as the nitrogen in the air brakes down. When corona occurs, it creates ozone (detrimental to the human lungs, eyes, etc.), ultraviolet light, nitric acid, electromagnetic emissions and sound.

Ozone is a strong, odorous gas that deteriorates rubber-based insulation. If moisture or high humidity conditions exist, nitric acids can also be formed that attack copper and other metals. The electromagnetic emission can be heard as interference on AM radios and the corona sound can be heard by the human ear and ultrasonic scanning devices.

Arcing

An electric arc, or arc discharge, is an electrical breakdown of a gas that produces a prolonged electrical discharge. Development of corona present Arcing.

Tracking

Tracking is the formation of partially conductive, typically carbonized, pathways on the surface of insulating materials by electrical breakdown. Development of Arcing can present tracking.

ULTRASONIC CONDITION-BASED LUBRICATION

Ultrasound innovation is ideally appropriate for condition-based oil techniques. With ultrasonic review instruments a program can be set up that will educate monitors which bearing should be greased up and help oil professionals realize precisely how much oil to apply.

To see how these instruments can function successfully in the loud environments of a run of the mill plant, one must comprehend the innovation of ultrasound, how ultrasound is produced by direction, and how ultrasound observing instruments can help keep up ideal oil levels in bearing.

The innovation depends on the detecting of high-recurrence sounds. Ultrasound is considered to begin at 20,000 cycles for each second, or 20 kilohertz (kHz). This is viewed as the high-recurrence edge at which human hearing stops. Most ultrasonic instruments utilized to screen hardware will detect from 20 kHz up to 100 kHz. The scope of human hearing spreads frequencies of from 20 cycles for every second (20 Hz) up to 20 kHz. The normal human will frequently hear up to 16.5 kHz and no more.

These recurrence correlations are critical to note on the grounds that there are contrasts in the manner low-recurrence and high-recurrence sounds travel, which assist us with understanding why ultrasound can be successfully established in bearing checking and oil programs.

Oiling Procedures

It is basic to think about two components of expected failure: absence of oil and over grease. Ordinary bearing burdens cause a versatile disfigurement of the components in the contact region giving a smooth circular circulation. Yet, bearing surfaces are not entirely smooth. Consequently, the genuine pressure appropriation in the contact zone will be influenced by an arbitrary surface harshness. Within the sight of a grease film on a heading surface, there is a hosing impact on the pressure conveyance, and the acoustic vitality delivered will be low. Should oil be diminished to a point where the pressure conveyance is not, at this point present, the typical unpleasant spots will connect with the face surfaces and increment the acoustic vitality. These ordinary infinitesimal distortions will start to deliver wear and the conceivable outcomes of little gaps may create which adds to the "pre-failure" condition. Accordingly, beside typical wear, the weakness or administration life of an orientation is firmly affected by the relative film thickness gave by a fitting ointment.

Staying away from Over Lubrication

At the point when an excessive amount of ointment is placed into the bearing lodging, pressure constructs up and can prompt an expansion of warmth, which can make pressure and disfigurement of the bearing. Or then again it can break or "pop" the bearing seal permitting grease to spill out into undesirable zones, (for example, an engine winding), or permit foreign substances to enter the raceway. All of which can prompt bearing failure.

The suitable measure of oil is significant. On the off chance that a bearing is over greased up the bearing can be pushed unnecessarily by the ointment causing extra wear of the bearing. Then again, if there isn't sufficient grease, the bearing will rub on the strong surface, again causing erosion and wear on the orientation. Either case is hindering to the life of the bearing. Utilizing airborne/structure borne ultrasound removes the speculation from grease.

Ultrasound Monitoring

Ultrasound instruments identify changes identified with contact. An appropriately greased up bearing will have next to no grating. The ointment levels out any pressure the bearing experiences as it moves around the raceway in this manner decreasing the potential for ruinous contact. As the bearing moves, it delivers a conspicuous "surging" sound much the same as the sound of air spilling out of a tire. This surging sound is alluded to as "background noise." incorporates all sounds, both low and high frequencies. The high-recurrence waves created by this background noise more restricted than those of the lower frequencies. Utilizing a ultrasonic interpreter, these signs can be identified with practically zero impedance from other mechanical commotions created by different parts, for example, a pole or another bearing close by. As the oil level in a heading falls or weakens, the potential for contact increments. There will be a relating ascend in the ultrasound adequacy level that can be noted and heard. The technique to decide when to grease up.

Furthermore, when to quit applying grease with ultrasound instruments is as straightforward as: setting a gauge, setting assessment timetables and checking as you grease up.

Setting up the greasing level:

A benchmark for an orientation reflects in decibels the level at which it is working under typical conditions with no detectable faults and with sufficient grease.

There are three techniques for setting a pattern

1. Examination: when there is more than one orientation of a similar sort, load what's more, rpm, various orientation can be contrasted one with the other. Each bearing is examined at a similar test point and edge. The decibel levels furthermore, stable quality is looked at. On the off chance that there are no considerable contrasts, (under 8dB) a pattern dB level is set for each bearing. This is normally performed with a compact ultrasonic interpreter.

2. Set while greasing up. While oil is being applied, tune in until the sound level drops down and starts to rise. By then no more oil is included and the dB esteem is utilized as the pattern.

3. Historical: bearing dB levels are gotten from an underlying review. After thirty days the bearing dB levels are taken and looked at. On the off chance that there is close to nothing (under 8dB) to no adjustment in dB than the benchmark levels are set and will be utilized for examination for resulting assessments.

Setting Inspection Schedules
This should be based on the equipment criticality, environment, type of industry, failure consequence, failure occurrence and the availability of standby. Typically one month is good. But for baring that have had significant levels and have been along these lines greased up, it may be important to test all the more habitually to take note of any potential changes.

Accessibility Problems

There might be circumstances in which it might be hard to access a few bearings. For instance, there might be a perplexing machine where a bearing is inserted in a territory where just a lubc tube is reached out external the packaging. On the off chance that the lube tube is a conductive metal, for example, copper, the bearing can even now be tried and a grease activity level set. On the off chance that the fitting is of a non-sound conductive material, for example, plastic, a different conductive metallic wave guide can be introduced so the bearing can be observed. The wave guide can be confined from structure borne clamor of the machine (the mounting point) through elastic disconnection material. Should it not be conceivable to put a wave manage, there is an elective arrangement. A transducer can be forever mounted on the bearing lodging and a link race to an opening. The link can be appended to a specific connector that can be "connected" to the ultrasonic sensor, as demonstrated as follows.

Auto Greaser and Ultrasound Sensor

Some systems prefer to use auto greasers for bearing. In this case installing an ultrasound sensor is a must to adjust the grease flow. The grease will be on and off based on the ultrasound sensor orders.

Conclusion

Ultrasound innovation is perfectly appropriate for viable condition-based grease programs. The short-wave nature of the sign diminishes obstruction from contending commotions and permits reviewers to precisely screen bearing condition. By setting up a caution level of 8 dB over a given benchmark, investigators will know when and when not to grease up. Over oil can be dodged by applying just enough grease to accomplish standard levels or tune in to a drop in the sound level should no dB reference be accessible.

MACHINE FAULTS DETECTION
USING ULTRASOUND

Please refer to this link for a complete set of sound tracks of the most common faults detects by ultrasound.

ULTRASOUND AND MEDICAL FIELD

Clinical ultrasound (otherwise called symptomatic sonography or ultrasonography) is a demonstrative imaging procedure, or remedial utilization of ultrasound. It is utilized to make a picture of inside body structures, for example, ligaments, muscles, joints, veins, and inward organs. The practice of examining pregnant women using ultrasound is called obstetric ultrasound, and was an early development and application of clinical ultrasonography.

An ultrasound can provide a view of the:

- Bladder.
- Brain (in infants).
- Eyes.
- Gallbladder.
- Kidneys.
- Liver.
- Ovaries.

- Pancreas.
- Spleen.
- Thyroid.
- Testicles.
- Uterus.
- Blood vessels.

While in maintenance we use an instrument to hear the faulty equipment, Ultrasonic images used in medical field, also known as sonograms, are made by sending pulses of ultrasound into tissue using a probe. The ultrasound pulses echo off tissues with different reflection properties and are recorded and displayed as an image.

Many different types of images can be formed. The most common is a B-mode image (Brightness), which displays the acoustic impedance of a two-dimensional cross-section of tissue. Other types can display blood flow, motion of tissue over time, the location of blood, the presence of specific molecules, the stiffness of tissue, or the anatomy of a three-dimensional region.

REFERENCES

Cormaik, M. & Ege, Y. 2017. Discontinuity Inspection in Pipelines: A Comparison Review. Measurement 111, 359-373.

Murphy, T. & Reinstra, A. 2010. Hear More A Guide to Using Ultrasound for Leak Detection and Condition Monitoring. Reliabilityweb.com; 1st Edition.

Soliman, M. H. A. 2020. Practical Guide to FMEA: A Proactive Approach to Failure Analysis. KDP.

Soliman, M. H. A. 2014. Analyzing Failure to Prevent Problems. Industrial Management 56(5), 10.

The Path to Lubrication Excellence – UE Systems.

UE Systems Lubrication E-Book.

UE Systems Energy E-Book.

ABOUT THE AUTHOR

Mohammed Hamed Ahmed Soliman is an industrial engineer, consultant, university lecturer, operational excellence leader, and author. He works as a lecturer at the American University in Cairo and as a consultant for several international industrial organizations.

Soliman earned a bachelor of science in Engineering and a master's degree in Quality Management. He earned post-graduate degrees in Industrial Engineering and Engineering Management. He holds numerous certificates in management, industry, quality, and cost engineering.

For most of his career, Soliman worked as a regular employee for various industrial sectors. This included crystal-glass making, fertilizers, and chemicals. He did this while educating people about the culture of continuous improvement.

Soliman has lectured at Princess Noura University and trained the maintenance team in Vale Oman Pelletizing Company. He has been lecturing at The American University in Cairo for 6 year and has designed and delivered 40 leadership and technical skills enhancement training modules.

Soliman is a member at the Institute of Industrial and Systems Engineers and a member with the Society for Engineering and Management Systems. He has published several articles in peer reviewed academic journals and magazines. His writings on lean manufacturing, leadership, productivity, and business appear in Industrial Engineers, Lean Thinking, and Industrial Management. Soliman's blog is www.personal-lean.org.

Also, by Mohammed Hamed Ahmed Soliman

https://www.amazon.com/-/e/B00NEY7BRE?fbclid=IwAR1ZM31VKzUyiytw5hKuzu3c9btnuPn08JOb2oA4PWE8h26G_jdG9Cqn2Ag

Recommended reads: